NO VACANCY

My story of domestic violence, murder, and the children caught in the crossfire

By Xiyya Jackson

TITLE: No Vacancy
By: Xiyya Jackson
Edited by: 846 Publishing
Cover Design: 846 Publishing
Copyright 2022

DEDICATION

The fight is not over...

I want to dedicate this book to my loving mother, Rosa Pearl Jackson — a beautiful, hard-working mother of 12 who lost her life at the hands of an abuser. It was because she lost her life as a result of domestic violence and the fact that I am a survivor of domestic violence that inspired me to write this book.

I love you, Mama.

The fight is not over...

PREFACE

*"Even when I stop crying, even when we fall asleep
and I'm nestled in his arms, this will leave another
scar. No one will see it. No one will know. But it will
be there. And eventually all of the scars will have
scars, and that's all I'll be--one big scar of a love
gone wrong."*

— *Amanda Grace, But I Love Him*

The day the father of my children died, I had to come to terms with
some cold, hard truths. There were dozens of realities I needed to
face. But three of them rose to the top like cream. The first was that
he wasn't the man I thought he was. The second was that my
children's lives would be changed forever. The third was that I was
capable of taking a life. He was dead, and I was the one who did it.

At the time I started writing this book, I was a 35-year-old single
mother of six: four boys and a set of twin girls. Their ages are 19,
13, 11, 11, 10, and 9. As I wrote these words, I was incarcerated in
the Marion County jail defending myself against a murder charge
since March of 2017.

I lived in an abusive relationship for years. I bore the marks of his
rage, anger, and exploitation on my body. But the bruises on my
body were nothing compared to the injury he did to my soul. He
broke everything about me: my finances, my self-esteem, and my
children.

I met my children's father in 2006. I was a young mother of two
children back then. I was pregnant with the twins. Vic and I would
later have two beautiful boys together. But the domestic violence

history that had plagued my family for decades would continue in my life. That dark road would lead to an even darker place: jail.

At the hand of my abuser, I have suffered stalking verbal emotional, physical, sexual, and digital abuse. I have been raped, kidnapped, beaten, tortured, and hospitalized. My harrowing tale is captured in the coming pages.

Abuse is like a hurricane. It destroys everything in its path. But it doesn't take the destruction away with the wind. Just as a hurricane lifts up houses and slams them back down to the ground, abuse doesn't sweep a woman away. It leaves behind all of the evidence that it was there. The pain. The shame. The hopelessness.

I never should have gotten involved with my abuser. The signs were there from the beginning. I should have known. It has been the source of my continual regret and a thousand questions why. Why did I not see who he was sooner? Why did I ever let him hit me? Why did I allow him to rape me again and again? Why did I return to him to be victimized? Why did his life have to be lost? Why would my children be without their father? And why would I have to spend time in jail for taking a life?

Abuse is a kind of murder in and of itself. It killed the best parts of me. It placed a veil over my face and darkened my outlook on the world. It killed what might have been a happy family with beautiful and smart children whose world was turned upside down when their mom went to jail and their dad went to the grave.

In the coming pages, you are going to read some of the most horrifying stories. You will walk with me on the journey back through the saddest and most desperate days of my life. But do not pity me. I don't desire your pity. I want your action. Why? Because in the few moments it took you to read this introduction, a woman was badly beaten by someone who claimed to love her, someone who should have wanted to protect her, someone who had been sexually intimate with her. In the past three minutes, some woman has lost her sense of security in the world as the man she loved and trusted used his strength and capitalized on her love to blacken her eye, force his genitals inside her, or break her arm. The world around her changed from a place of light and love and became a world that was scary and uncertain.

The cycle of victimizing has to end and a cycle of healing, education, and support has to begin. It has to start with you and me. We have to raise our voices so that women know their worth and little girls understand that they don't deserve anything but the best.

I didn't know who I was. So, I let a man who was incapable of true love define who I was. He did it with his fists and with the many other ways he took my life from me.

Yes, he lost his life. But so did I. And so did our children.
There is a lot of work to do. It starts with reading this book and then sharing it with someone who might be suffering at the hand of someone they love right now. Buckle your seatbelts. We are in for a bumpy ride.

According to the National Council Against Domestic Violence:

- 20 people per minute are physically abused by an intimate partner in the United States.

- 1 in 4 women experience severe intimate partner physical violence, intimate partner sexual violence, and/or intimate partner stalking.

- 1 in 3 women have experienced slapping, shoving, pushing) and in some cases might not be considered "domestic violence."

- 1 in 7 women have been injured by an intimate partner.

- 1 in 10 women have been raped by an intimate partner.

- 1 in 4 women have been victims of severe physical violence (e.g., beating, burning, strangling) by an intimate partner.

- 1 in 7 women have been stalked by an intimate partner to the point in which they felt very fearful or believed that they or someone close to them would be harmed or killed.

- On a typical day, there are more than 20,000 phone calls placed to domestic violence hotlines nationwide.

Domestic violence is real. I am living evidence of how it can set a life off track and leave a woman fighting for her existence and for her children's future. The cost is high. But prevention is the cure. Women need to learn to love and respect themselves while teaching that same lesson to their daughters and teaching their sons healthy ways to love.

"Never let a man put his hands on you without your permission in any capacity, to love you, to hurt you, to restrain you. Your body must be seen as your domain, your kingdom, you place of peace and safety. If anyone is to touch that special and private place, they can only do so by invitation.

TABLE OF CONTENTS

Chapter 1 – Blood in the lobby

"Your abusive partner doesn't have a problem with his anger; he has a problem with your anger. One of the basic human rights he takes away from you is the right to be angry with him. No matter how badly he treats you, he believes that your voice shouldn't rise and your blood shouldn't boil. The privilege of rage is reserved for him alone. When your anger does jump out of you—as will happen to any abused woman from time to time—he is likely to try to jam it back down your throat as quickly as he can. Then he uses your anger against you to prove what an irrational person you are. Abuse can make you feel straitjacketed. You may develop physical or emotional reactions to swallowing your anger, such as depression, nightmares, emotional numbing, or eating and sleeping problems, which your partner may use as an excuse to belittle you further or make you feel crazy."

— Lundy Bancroft, Why Does He Do That? Inside the minds of angry and controlling men

* *

As I stood there watching the blood pour from Vincent's body, I wondered what could have happened to him. Why was he laying on the ground? Why was the hotel staff screaming and running? Why was I in this hotel at all? Why is there blood... so much blood?

For a long time, I couldn't remember anything that happened just moments earlier when I retrieved my handgun from my purse and shot the father of my children in the lobby of our neighborhood hotel. I had briefly slipped outside of my body and seemed to be floating over the scene like a spectator at a play.

Abuse is a strange tonic. It leaves you intoxicated and unable to judge reality from fiction. It makes you think that hitting is loving. It breaks you down as a person on the inside so that you are less of a human being. The abuser becomes larger than life as you start to shrink away as a person. Before long, you don't know who you are, what you believe, and what you shouldn't accept.

The worst part about abuse is how it breaks your self-confidence. You start to believe that, because of what you've been through, because of the scars on your face, the scars on your body, and the scars on your heart, no one else will see any value in you. No one else will want you. You are damaged beyond repair, or so you think. So, you cling to the abuser as your last hope for companionship.

It locks women into a cycle that seems to have no escape hatch. That is where I was on that fateful day. It was the perfect storm: an abusive man, a victimized woman, no one to help, and a loaded gun.

A lot of lives were changed that day. If only someone would have listened the many times when I cried out for help. If only I had followed through when help was given. If only we had never even met. Now a life is gone. Families are mourning. Children are without parents. And I was fearing 65 years in prison.

I wished I had a way to talk to women before they started dating the very first time. I wished I could let them know that they matter. I wished I could scream from the rooftops that one thing that would have saved my life: love is not abuse and abuse is not love.

I did not know that. All I ever knew was that the men who claimed to love the women in my life also tortured them. I chose someone who confirmed that theory. Now, there was blood on the floor.

Chapter 2 – How it all began

"One of the obstacles to recognizing chronic mistreatment in relationships is that most abusive men simply don't seem like abusers. They have many good qualities, including times of kindness, warmth, and humor, especially in the early period of a relationship. An abuser's friends may think the world of him. He may have a successful work life and have no problems with drugs or alcohol. He may simply not fit anyone's image of a cruel or intimidating person. So when a woman feels her relationship spinning out of control, it is unlikely to occur to her that her partner is an abuser."

— Lundy Bancroft, Why Does He Do That?: Inside the Minds of Angry and Controlling Men

* *

When I was born, I was given the name Xiyya. (I have a niece named Xiyya as well.) It is a unique name. In fact, I have never met another person with the same name. That is fitting since I have never met another person with my story. I have been all the way to hell on a one-way ticket. But I somehow made it back. The man who drove me to the depths of hell was the man I once loved and adored. He was the father of two of my children. I never wanted any harm to come to him. I always wanted the best for him and myself as individuals and as a couple. And I certainly never wanted to see him die.

The cycle of violence began between my significant other and myself long before we met. When I was just ten years old, tragedy struck my family. My mother was killed by her boyfriend. All I knew, as a young girl, is that they left together to go to the store. To pick up something she was missing for our Thanksgiving dinner. She never came home.

It was clear that they got into an altercation. Rather than face justice for hurting her, he chose to kill her and throw her body in White River near our home. My mother's body wasn't found for three months when it surfaced.

When she first went missing, we were hopeful that she would be discovered and returned to us. But as the days turned to weeks and weeks turned to months, our hope faded.

The man who killed her got a slap on the wrist. He only served two years.

Domestic Violence is a parasite. Once it attaches to a family, it can spread and grow, touching the children and the children's children for generations to come. That is why it must be seriously addressed. I witnessed abuse toward my mother and all ten of my sisters. The cycle of violence was never broken, so it made its way to me.

I met Victor, who I lovingly referred to as Vic, in 2006 in Lafayette Indiana when I was pregnant with my twin girls. It was a rough time for me. I was about to be the mother of two children at the same time. I was going to have to navigate the financial and emotional struggles that come with giving birth to twins. There were some things I knew about having twins. I was a twin myself and there were plenty of twins running through my family. But visiting my twin nieces or cousins was one thing; living with twins, raising them, and caring for them all by myself was another. I was feeling anxious to say the least.

Meeting Vic seemed like a stroke of luck. He was funny, smart, and cool. He was from Chicago, Illinois and came to Lafayette with his then-girlfriend. That is where he met my cousin, Ashley, as she was walking through my apartment complex. She was great at meeting people and striking up an instant friendship. She brought Vic to my apartment and introduced us. Since I was pregnant, I wasn't looking for a love interest. In fact, all I wanted from him was a ride to the store. But his charm and helpfulness were irresistible.

He went with me to the store and then stayed with me for the rest of the day. He didn't seem at all bothered by the fact that I was pregnant. We were just drawn to each other, and he never wanted to leave my side. And I was happy to have someone interested in asking me how I was feeling other than my gynecologist! I was flattered by his constant attention, and his presence made me feel secure.

In those early days, he said all the right things. He scratched something that itched deep down in my heart. I wanted to be special and important to someone. Vic met that need. And he was able to carve out a place for himself in my heart.

It wasn't long before our relationship turned from friendship to caretaker-patient to physical. We started having sex on an almost daily basis. Being with him made me feel like I was the only person in his life that mattered to him. Then I found out that he had a girlfriend.

Vic had come to Indiana with his girlfriend in search of low-cost housing through a program that the state of Indiana was offering. But she was getting angry that he was away all of the time not knowing that he was spending his time with me. He made the decision to break up with her and put her on a bus back to Chicago so that he could be with me. I foolishly thought that was sweet and charming.

His romantic game was strong. In the beginning, he was drowning me with gifts, attention, affection, and sex. He started selling drugs and paying bills so that I could focus on my big task: giving birth to twins. On October 24th, three months before my due date, I went into labor. The doctors determined that I needed to go through with the delivery rather than try to slow down the labor. My twin girls were born three months early. They immediately went into the neonatal intensive care unit and had to stay in the hospital for three extra months until they were strong enough to be released.

I was overwhelmed. It was already going to be hard to care for twins. But caring for twins who were tiny and in need of constant care was more than I could bear. The doctors advised me that, if I was going to take them home, I would need to change their feeding tubes frequently. The hospital insisted that at least one other person know how to change the feeding tubes. Guess who volunteered? Vic! He came to the hospital and got the training so that he could help me with my new babies.

I was shocked at his kindness and willingness to help. I had not even asked him to do it. These weren't his children and we had only been together for a short time. But he stepped up to the plate and helped out, allowing me to bring my twins home.

Chapter 3 – The Tide Turns

"No amount of me trying to explain myself was doing any good. I didn't even know what was going on inside of me, so how could I have explained it to them?"

— *Sierra D. Waters, Debbie.*

* *

It didn't take long for the honeymoon to end. He transformed, over time, from a loving caring partner to a controlling maniac. The first sign of real trouble occurred a couple months after the twins came home. I wanted to take the kids to see my family in Indianapolis, but he didn't want me to go. He got angry for what I felt was no reason at all. He began to scream and curse me like a madman. I could not understand his position since all he would say was that he didn't want me to go. I thought he was going crazy. So, I went anyway.

That was the start of a cycle that would morph into years of abuse and end in his death. Little did I know then that we were setting off on a dangerous path down a dark and deadly road. How could I have known? Everything wasn't always bad between us. There were times when he was gentle and loving. There were dates to nice restaurants and spending time having fun. There were nights spent snuggled together on the couch watching television. But the good times started to dwindle and the wild, manic behavior started to increase. Before long, the bad outweighed the good.

Vic had a lot of people fooled. They were drawn in by his winsome personality and overwhelming charm just like I was. He was beloved by our friends and family and lured them in by buying them gifts and giving away money like it was nothing. I had people fooled too that I was happy and well taken care of by him. No one knew that behind closed doors, Vic was nothing like the public persona he showed the world.

The verbal and emotional abuse worsened to the point where I could hardly stand the sound of him coming through the door. But the worst was yet to come. The abuse would turn physical and become violent against me and against my children.

Chapter 4 – Hard to Believe

"The abusive man's high entitlement leads him to have unfair and unreasonable expectations, so that the relationship revolves around his demands. His attitude is: "You owe me." ...He wants his partner to devote herself fully to catering to him, even if it means that her own needs—or her children's—get neglected. You can pour all your energy into keeping your partner content, but if he has this mind-set, he'll never be satisfied for long. And he will keep feeling that you are controlling him, because he doesn't believe that you should set any limits on his conduct or insist that he meet his responsibilities.... When she stands up to him, he makes her pay for it—sooner or later. Friends say: "Leave him." But she knows it won't be that easy. He will promise to change... He'll get severely depressed, causing her to worry whether he'll be all right. And, depending on what style of abuser he is, she may know that he will become dangerous when she tries to leave him. She may even be concerned that he will try to take her children away from her, as some abusers do."

— Lundy Bancroft, Why Does He Do That?: Inside the Minds of Angry and Controlling Men

* *

When I look back over the events of my life, I often wonder what I might have done differently. I think about what I might have said to people to get them to offer more support or help me out of my situation. But the reality is that people are not well equipped to handle a woman's complaints of domestic violence especially when they are close to the person she claims to be her abuser. People didn't believe a lot of things that I would tell them.

I started feeling desperate. It was hard to know exactly what would set Vic off. In the beginning, it seemed like we would have a disagreement that turned into an argument. The argument would result in him slapping me or kicking me. But, over time, seemingly insignificant things were enough to make him lose his mind and put his hands on me. I felt I had no recourse; I promised myself that, if it happened again, I would call the police.

The first time the cops came into my home, handcuffed my boyfriend and took him away was one of the worst days in my life. My emotions vacillated between relief that I wouldn't be hit again that night and the worry about being responsible for sending him to jail. But the police could see my black eyes, bruised cheeks, and marks all over my body. They had to take him away.

He would stay in jail for a couple of days and return to my home apologetically. I would acquiesce and let him back in. Once, his stay in jail was extended. I was used to our old pattern where he would beat me up, get arrested, stay in jail for a few days and then come knocking at my door. So, when he didn't show after a couple of days, I started to worry about him. It turned out that he had drug charges that came up when he was arrested for domestic violence. So, they kept him on those charges.

Still, I took him back knowing that the beatings would get worse and worse. I started to fear for my life, my children's lives, and Vic's future if he killed me and went to jail for life. Sure enough, the beatings intensified until, one day, he nearly beat me to death. I ended up in the hospital for several days forcing me to be away from my children who needed my care. And, they were emotionally scarred from seeing me get beat to the point that an ambulance had to come and carry me away. They were scarred further by the fear and terror of their mother being in the hospital. Their young minds had no way to process this drama. So, they just wallowed in fear.

Once, as was my custom, I bonded him out of jail after beating me. We went home and he jumped on me the same day and ended up back in jail — all within a 24-hour period.

Today, it is easy to look back and see that I was a broken woman to allow a man to treat me the way he did and put my life in constant jeopardy. But back then, it wasn't all so clear.

Vic was a good provider. By the time our relationship was solidified, I had six children. Their care and my ability to provide for their futures were the most important thing on my mind. Vic was a good provider. He always took good care of me and my kids. We had two children together in addition to the four I had when our relationship began. But he did not distinguish between the children. He took care of all of the children whether they were his biological kids or not. He paid all the rent and bills month after month so that I did not have to worry.

But the money he provided came at a price. He felt that it gave him the right to run my life. He was controlling and abusive. I knew that it had to stop. I had to find my way out. I had to figure out a way to support myself and live alone without his help. But how?

Chapter 5 – The Last Straw

"A real man busts his ass to feed his family, fights for them if he has to, dies for them if he has to. And he treats his wife with respect every day of his life, treats her like a queen - the queen of the home she makes for their children."

— *S.M. Stirling, Dies the Fire*

* *

The first time Vic came to my house, he was friendly and charming. He went with me to meet my oldest son as he got off the bus. After I introduced Vic to my son, they said hello. But my son had something else pressing on his mind:

"Mom, there is a book fair at school. I need some money."

"I'm sorry, sweetie. I don't have any extra money," I answered.

"How much do you need, little man?" Vic asked.

My son's eyes lit up. "$25, sir."

Vic reached in his pocket, pulled out a $5 and $20 bill, and proudly handed them to my son.

"You let me know if you need more, OK, buddy?"

"Yes sir!" my son said enthusiastically.

That was one of the ways Vic lured me into the relationship. He knew that we were financially destitute. So, I would trade him sex for money. I wasn't a prostitute; but we were both getting something to get something. He wanted sex. I wanted his love.
He started coming over my house more and staying longer until he was practically living with us.

One day, I was nearly due to have our first son. My twins were still young. And Vic and I were getting closer and closer because of all the help he provided me. But when we started fighting, it seemed that everything turned quite drastically.

It all started when Vic got his hands on a supply of Ecstasy pills that he thought he could sell. He decided that he would go to the strip club to sell the pills. While he was there, though, he got friendly with one of the strippers. He walked in the door that night with this woman following close behind him. I was surprised. He introduced us. I tried to be polite and say hello, but I asked him why this person, who was obviously a stripper judging by the way she was dressed, was in my home. He informed me that he brought the stripper home thinking we were going to have a threesome.

"No!" I shouted and turned to walk away from him.

He picked up a glass and swung at me. I turned around just in time to see the glass coming toward my face. I threw my hand up to block the strike. He hit my wrist and I heard it snap.

This was the cycle of violence we lived with day after day. Our fights became louder and his attacks became more violent. The children's screams along with my own rang throughout the neighborhood. I should not have been shocked when Child Protective Service (CPS) workers showed up at my door, gathered up all six children, and took them all away. Now, a new battle had begun. I had to work to regain custody.

The courts ordered several classes and other requirements like a full-time job. Vic was banned from the home. I left the court distraught over having to find work. Who would hire me with a broken wrist?

Not to mention, who would want me working in their company with the bruises all over my arms and legs and the black eyes Vic had given me. I went home with Vic and a broken heart. Since I could not have my kids, I decided the least I could have was my abuser. We fused together in a vicious cycle. We were both broken inside and needed the drama we created together.

He tried to cheer me up as if he understood that he was partially responsible for the loss of my kids. He encouraged me to put in some application and even helped me put makeup on to cover the black eyes bruises and scratches. Whenever the CPS workers would stop by the house for a visit, he would take off running before I answered the door because he wasn't supposed to be in the house at all. He would run down the stairs to hide in the basement.

After several visits and lots of hoops to jump through, I was allowed to have my kids back. But I knew that if I was going to have any chance at a life for them and myself, I needed to get away from Vic.

Chapter 6 – The Big Move

"I am living in hell from one day to the next. But there is nothing I can do to escape. I don't know where I would go if I did. I feel utterly powerless, and that feeling is my prison. I entered of my own free will, I locked the door, and I threw away the key."

— Haruki Murakami

* *

Vic took every opportunity he could to come back to Indianapolis and stay connected to my family or people I was close to. He would invite them to parties or offer them drugs — any excuse he could find to be Indianapolis.

One year in March, he came down a couple days before his birthday to pay for a party for my son. So, I went to the party and then stayed with him at the hotel afterward. It was a big mistake. When it was time to leave, we got in his car. He was pretending to take me home. But then he started heading toward Lafayette, taking me against my will. Besides, I was starving and kept asking him to get off the highway, so I could eat.

All the while, I was secretly texting my sister from another phone I had in my purse. When we pulled off the highway to go into a Mexican restaurant, I saw my chance. I ordered my food, but I stayed there long enough for the police to come and get me away from him. I kept procrastinating and trying to buy time because I knew the police were coming. When I couldn't stall any longer inside the store, we walked outside. But I walked as slowly as I could. Thankfully, the police were pulling up. Vic took off running. A few weeks later, he started calling my phone. He claimed he wanted to talk to the kids but never did. He always tried to keep me on the phone. So, I stopped answering his calls. That made him call even more. One day, I had more than ninety missed calls from him. The day after I got my kids back and my case was closed, I headed for the local U-Haul store. I rented a truck and started loading up all of my possessions to go back to Indiana. I was escaping my abuser, I thought. But I forgot to leave my abuser behind. He went with me to the U-Haul store and rented the truck because I didn't have the money to do so. But the whole time, he was raging that I shouldn't move. I continued to forge ahead. After I loaded it up with whatever I could fit in it, he stood on the sidewalk threatening to burn it up because I was leaving him.

I listened to his rants as I drove away. After I got to Indianapolis, Indiana and got settled, I found out I was pregnant with another child by Vic. It would be our second son together. Vic came to Indianapolis from time to time threatening me, harassing me, or begging me to take him back in.

One day, I came home and found him lurking inside my garage. I would never know when he was going to show up. In another instance, it was evening and I was pulling out from my driveway. I looked back and saw that he was driving in a vehicle behind me. I rode down my street trying to think of a way to outmaneuver him. But he hit my car from behind at high speed. The car went flying and flipped in the air, smashing into a truck parked on the street.

I came to rest on the side of the road, dazed and confused. Just then, my car door opened and I felt Vic's powerful hands on my chest as he dragged me out the car, threw me to the ground, and stomped me in my stomach — all this while I was pregnant with his child.

As I laid there on the ground, all of my regrets bubbled to the surface. The reality was that I had allowed the thread that connected us to remain intact. I had moved to escape him. But then I behaved in ways that did not sever the ties between us. I let him know where

I lived. I kept accepting his phone calls. I failed to show up for court when he was being tried for his abuse of me.

It is hard to explain the emotions that drove my decisions. There were so many. Of course, there was guilt. He always made me feel sad for him when it was time for him to face justice for his crimes. I also still loved him. And there was fear… always fear.

One day, he stole a car from Lafayette and came to Indiana with the intention of kidnapping our youngest son. He was successful in taking him, but for some reason, he didn't keep him. He dropped him off at a fire station in Chicago.

All along, his mental issues and his buried rage were showing me that he was a man to be feared and avoided at all costs. But I kept leaving the door cracked open, and that was all he needed to make his way back in time after time.

Once, when we had a confrontation, I got the strength and will to fight back. But it seemed that fighting back did cause him to back down. Instead, it made him bolder and stronger. I punched and kicked trying to get him away from me. It seemed to turn him into a mad dog. He responded by biting. He bit me all over my body. He chomped down on my finger and bit through the bone on my finger. When I got to the hospital, I had bite marks in several spots on my body. My finger was permanently deformed, and I would wear his bite marks on my breast and arms for the rest of my life.

In another instance when I gave in and took him back, we got in a car together to take a drive. An argument erupted during the ride and I asked to get out. He refused to let me out and started driving faster and more erratically. I opened the passenger door and jumped out of the moving car trying to get away from him.

The cycle of abuse continued and intensified. He came to the house one day raging about something. It turned into a physical altercation and he beat me terribly in front of my children. When I begged him to stop and threatened to call 911, he snatched my phone and ran.

It was no longer safe for me and my kids to remain at the house in Lafayette. I packed up my clothes and my children and rushed to a domestic violence shelter to get away from him. The shelter gave me a phone that could call 911 so I could feel safe when I left the shelter.

Chapter 7 – From Abuse to Abduction

"Has he ever trapped you in a room and not let you out? Has he ever raised a fist as if he were going to hit you? Has he ever thrown an object that hit you or nearly did? Has he ever held you down or grabbed you to restrain you?

Has he ever shoved, poked, or grabbed you?

Has he ever threatened to hurt you?

If the answer to any of these questions is yes, then we can stop wondering whether he'll ever be violent; he already has been."

— Lundy Bancroft, Why Does He Do That?: Inside the Minds of Angry and Controlling Men

* *

"Hey, it's me," Vic's voice said on my phone.

"What? What do you want?"

"I want to see the kids. I have stuff for them!"

"No, you don't," I answered. "You want to see me so you can beat on me some more."

"No, I swear. I just want to see them. Please, Xiyya."

"I can't let you come to my house anymore, Vic."

"Ok, fine, then. I'll meet you somewhere."

"The church. I'll meet you in the parking lot of the church."

Meeting at the church parking lot was the place where I felt the most safe. There, he couldn't control me. And he couldn't beat me without someone seeing it and intervening or, at least, calling the cops. It brought a degree of normalcy to our relationship as parents. But I was soon to learn that the sense of normalcy was a dangerous thing.

We started talking and behaving civilly to each other. With the threat of violence. First, we talked. Then we laughed. In time, we were back together. I fell for his crap again when he said he wanted to have sex. He even offered to pay me large sums of money to sleep with him. I was desperate and weak, so I agreed. I needed companionship as much as I needed money. The sex was good... so was the cash.

We would usually go to a hotel because I still did not trust inside the confines of my house. But a deadly pattern was starting to develop. When it was time for me to leave to go home, he started acting crazy. We would have sex all night long. Then, in the morning, he wanted to have sex again before I left. If I refused, he would turn violent.

Each time we got together, it got worse and worse, so I decided that I wouldn't have sex with him anymore. When he asked why, I told him I had an STD. His response was, "I don't care if I get an STD as long as it came from you."

I stayed strong and stayed away from him for quite some time. Then one day, he showed up at my home. I would not let him in. He asked if I would come out and talk to him. I wish I had been strong and slammed the door in his face. But I went to the curb to talk to him. That's when he grabbed me and threw me in his car holding the lock button down on the key fob so I couldn't get out. Then he ran around to the driver's door and got in. I fought him from the passenger side while he got the car started and sped away leaving my children in the house behind.

This pattern of kidnapping continued a few more times. Each time, he took me away farther and kept me away longer. One day, he came to the house under the pretense of wanting to talk. In reality, he just wanted to take me away. When I refused to go, he dragged me by my hair down the street. I was glad to not be thrown into a car. At least, out in the open, someone would hear and see. I held out hope that by the time he got me to the end of the block, the police would be on their way.

No such luck. He got me all the way down the street holding onto my hair like a caveman as I screamed and kicked and writhed, trying to get away. Then he dragged me around the corner to a street where some of the homes were abandoned. My heart rate, which was already speeding, went several beats faster because I knew I would be harder to find on this street.

I would hear barking as the sounds of our struggle passed house after house with dogs in the yard. He continued to drag me as my strength started to fail. I continued to scream but my voice was hoarse and my throat was raw.

He dragged me through an alley. By this time, my shoes had come off. I cried out that my feet hurt from the rocks on the bare soles of my feet. He took off his shoes and put them on me. He took me into the back of some abandoned duplexes where he called a female friend of his to come get us.

Shortly after, she showed up, and we both got in the back seat. He had her get a hotel room in her name. She left us there in the room together.

Once I knew he was asleep, I ran to the front office to call my kids. I could hear them crying and screaming in terror from not knowing where I was. A detective got on the phone asking where I was.

Minutes later, police arrive. A female detective walked up to me. It was clear that she was not happy at all about the situation. She asked if I remembered a case back in 1992 where a mother of 12 went missing. I said, "Yes, she was my mom." The detective said, "I worked your mom's case. And I was scared I would be looking for your body the same way I was looking for your mother's body."

She sent the other officers up to the hotel room to find him, but he was gone, sparking a hunt. He was found under a truck at a restaurant next door.

Weeks later, I was subpoenaed to court, but I didn't show up. I still could not bring myself to testify against him and put him away for years and years. But the court did not appreciate my decision to be absent. The judge sent three police cars to my house to get me. When I arrived at court, the judge addressed me.

"Ms. Jackson, I wanted to talk to you personally. You filed these charges and then elected not to testify. We will not tolerate your abuse of the court system. I will hold you in contempt and have you arrested if you don't show up for the next hearing. This man is being tried rape among other chargers. And because you chose not to show, we have to reschedule. I have lost my patience with you. Do you understand?"

"Yes, your Honor," I answered sheepishly.

But as I was leaving the courtroom, I was told that because I didn't show up, Vic ended up signing a plea that dropped most of his charges. He was only given a sentence of two or three years. And it was all my fault.

As Mother's Day was approaching, Vic reached out to me again. This time, he was trying to tell me that he wanted to celebrate me as a mother and give me a nice day. I let him come over the day before Mother's Day and we spent some time together, but I would not let him stay over. He went to spend the night with a friend of his.

The next morning, he came back to my house shirtless and already filled with rage, demanding to be let in. When I told him he had to leave, he got angry. He grabbed me and pulled me out the house before punching me in the face repeatedly. I prayed that someone would see what was going on while praying that my children would not see what was going on.

He started dragging me down the street and around the corner just as he had done before. All the while, he kept hitting me in my face. I wasn't sure where I was because I was disoriented and he had been dragging me and punching me for so long. I thought we were blocks and blocks away. But we had only gone a short distance on a neighboring street.

As he dragged me down the street, he spotted a car sitting in front of someone's house. He forced me into the car even though it wasn't his. It was a beautiful, classic car that had been restored. There were t-shirts over the seats celebrating the car's make and model.

Having pushed me into the back seat, he held me there against my will. It was burning up hot on that summer day with the doors closed and the windows up. I was begging to be let go. I kept screaming that I was hot and wanted to go. So, he got in my face and blew on me with his mouth and fanned me with his hand while telling me that I was not going anywhere. Then he forced my skirt up and pushed himself inside me.

I could hear sirens blaring and dogs barking. He wanted to run because he knew a squadron of police were looking for me and, judging by the sirens, they were getting close. He pulled me out of the car and dragged me across the street into an abandoned house. The grass was high and the house looked like something from a horror movie. There were piles of trash in the yard and broken windows everywhere.

He pushed me down below the high grass to hide from the police as the sounds of the sirens got even closer. He worried that we might still be visible, so he dragged me around to the back of the house, broke the back windows, and forced me inside.

He had stolen one of the shirts from the car because he did not have a shirt on. He put it on and sat down beside me in the dark and dirty house. Everything around me was nasty and dirty. We sat there in silence broken only by his threats to kill me if I screamed out. I could hear that the police were just outside. The sound of the sirens was right in front of us and the dogs were barking wildly. Helicopters spun overhead shaking the rickety old house.

Suddenly we heard the sound of movement rustling through the grass. The dog must have picked up my scent after about 30 minutes. The police kicked in the door and the dogs attacked Vic. I don't know how they were trained to know who was the perpetrator and who was the victim. But they were charging directly for him. He jumped up and tried to jump out the window, but the dogs dragged him down to the ground.

A female police officer took me to the hospital. I was sobbing, but I was happy to be free. I was certain that he would have killed me that day. The nurse did a rape kit on me and Vic was charged with rape, criminal confinement, and strangulation.

As for me, I just wanted to get back home to kids who were thrilled to see me and terrified by all that happened.

Chapter 8 – I Shot Vic

"In a healthy relationship, vulnerability is wonderful. It leads to increased intimacy and closer bonds. When a healthy person realizes that he or she hurt you, they feel remorse and they make amends. It's safe to be honest. In an abusive system, vulnerability is dangerous. It's considered a weakness, which acts as an invitation for more mistreatment. Abusive people feel a surge of power when they discover a weakness. They exploit it, using it to gain more power. Crying or complaining confirms that they've poked you in the right spot."

— *Christina Enevoldsen, The Rescued Soul: The Writing Journey for the Healing of Incest and Family Betrayal*

* *

When I came to myself, I was standing in the lobby of the hotel — my personal heartbreak hotel — holding a gun in one hand and a phone in the other. I was talking to my adult son.

"I shot Vic," I heard myself say. In that moment, it all became real to me. My mind started to wander back to those days in Lafayette. Like a movie flashback, I played the scenes of meeting Vic. I could see in our low-income apartment having fun, watching movies, shopping, and hanging out.

I remembered the first time I saw him when my cousin introduced us. I felt that same feeling I felt then. I didn't like him at first. But my feelings grew. All of those feelings were backing up on me now, and I had no idea what I was supposed to do with them all. I started to shake inside and the room started to spin.

"How did I get here," I asked myself again. Finally, my mind was ready to answer the question and allow me to recall what had happened over the past two days that led to this point.

Vic had been calling for a couple days asking me to spend time with him for his birthday. I didn't want to spend time with him because I knew he wasn't good for me. Besides, every time I gave in to him, something bad happened. We would get into an argument, he would take me someplace and hold me hostage, or he would beat me up. I knew that even if we had fun, it would get bad whenever it was time for him to leave or time for me to leave.

He continued to beg and play on my emotions. He didn't want to be alone on his birthday. After a long conversation, he broke me down and I said yes. But I was at least smart enough to insist on one condition: I would only go if someone else could come along to make sure things didn't get out of hand.

I called my friend Re-Re and asked her to go with me. I thought he would not act out in front of her. We agreed to meet someplace later. Instead, he showed up at my house. He came to my house.

"What are you doing here?" I asked.

"Let me in!"

"No, Vic. You know you can't be in here. My kids are here." I knew that my oldest son, in particular, had been traumatized by all of the fighting. Plus, Vic had punched him in the stomach once when he tried to intervene to protect me.

"Come on, baby. Don't leave me lonely like that on my birthday. At least let's get a hotel room."

"Ok," I sighed. "Go get a room and just let me know where it is. Re-Re and I will come up there."

He left and got the room. So Re-Re and I went to the hotel. We broke out some alcohol and started drinking. Everything was good and we were having a great time. We sat around talking about old memories and having some laughs.

Then there was a knock on the door. In walked some of his junkie friends. I couldn't tell if Vic was buying or selling. But after they left, everything changed. Vic started to get more sullen and Re-Re decided it was time to go. She stood up to leave.

"You, OK, girl?!"

I looked around. The night had been calm and fun. "Yeah, girl. I'm cool." I watched as she walked out the door wondering if I had made the right decision. He had been on his best behavior, but I didn't know if that was because of his birthday or because we were being chaperoned.

But I let her leave. She lived in a different county and had a long drive home. I was hopeful things would stay calm. A little while later, I laid across the bed and went to sleep.
We did not even have sex which was strange for us. When I woke up in the morning, I was ecstatic that we had enjoyed a normal evening together without drama, without violence, and without sex.

I got ready to leave. There was going to be a talent show at the Boys and Girls Club and my children were performing. We were all very excited to see their act.

"Where are you going?" Vic barked.

Immediately, my heart started to pound. I knew that tone of voice meant trouble.

"I have to go. The kids have a talent show."

"No, I don't want you to leave."

"I have to go. The kids…"

"Will you come back?"

"No, Vic. I only agreed to come for your birthday. That was yesterday. I need to go."

He jumped to his feet and rushed over to the door blocking.

"Come on, now, Vic. We have had such a good time. Don't start this."

He got in my face. "I'm not letting you leave unless you promise to come back."

I kept saying no, but he would not let me out of the hotel room. I finally lied. "OK, fine. I will come back. I promise. You have to let me out now. I'm going to be late."

"You're a liar! You're not coming back!" He picked me up and carried me over to the bed. He slammed me down on the bed and held me with one hand while he reached for his phone with the other.

"What are you doing!" I screamed. "Who are you calling?"

"I'm calling Rockett. You know him."

Just then Rockett picked up.

"Yo, man. This Vic. You know your girl Xiyya. Well, I'm having sex with her right now," he said, jamming his fingers into my vagina. "Well, you can't have her. She belongs to me."

I screamed at the top of my lungs. "Stop Vic. Let me out of here."

I could hear Rockett yelling on the other hand asking why Vic was doing this. Then Rockett started yelling out for me. "Xiyya!! Where are you?! I'll come get you! Just scream out the name of the place where you are!"

I started to tell him, but I didn't want Rockett to come because Vic had a gun. Rockett was my good friend, and I didn't want anything to happen to him. So, I kept struggling and fighting Vic to let me leave. Finally, he let me up.

I ran to the door. But he got there at the same time.

"I don't trust you to come back, so I'm going with you. That way, I can make sure you come back."

I decided I would let him come with me because that was the only way to get away from him. We drove to the house. As soon as we pulled into the driveway, the kids ran out to meet Vic. My nephew, who had been staying with me that day, also came out to see him. While he was saying hello to them, I ran inside to shower and get ready.

When I came out of the shower, the house was eerily silent. There wasn't a sound anywhere. I knew something was wrong. In a house full of six kids, plus an extra relative, the house was hardly silent during the daylight hours. I rushed around the house looking for everyone. Then I ran to the window and looked out. His car was gone. He had taken the kids and my nephew.

I decided not to panic hoping that he had taken them to drop them off at the Boys and Girls Club. I didn't believe he would have done anything to hurt the children. But I feared he would try to keep me imprisoned at the house. I ran in the room and got dressed. As soon as I finished dressing, I heard the car engine. He had returned. The kids were gone, but he had my three-year old nephew.

Vic parked on the street instead of pulling into the driveway. My nephew came running toward me with all of his belongings — his sippy cup, his baby wipes and a couple of pullups. I ran toward him to help. Just then, Vic jumped out of the car and ran toward me. He grabbed me and my nephew and threw us in the truck. I didn't struggle hoping that he was taking me to the Boys & Girls club.

At the stop sign, he turned right toward the hotel instead of left toward the Club. Once he got there, he parked in the fire lane.

"Vic! What are you doing? I have to get to the club to see the kids."

"No!" he answered maniacally. "We need to get a room."

He came over to my side and pulled me out leaving my nephew behind. He whispered in my ear. "Just book the room and we will go to the club. Then I will know you are coming back." He pushed me toward the front door of the lobby.

I went inside pretending that I wanted to book the room. But, in reality, I was going inside to try to get help. But I heard his footsteps following behind me. My heart raced in fear for my three-year-old nephew left alone in the car.

I started talking to the front desk clerk as normally as I could. But I knew I needed to get Vic away from me so I could tell them to call the police.

"Go wait with him in the car," I said, hoping he would stay. But he returned in what felt like seconds with my nephew in tow.
Then I got an idea. I started searching my purse. "Vic," I said. "Can you get my phone charger out of the car? I need to plug in my phone. It's almost dead and the kids might try to call."

While he was gone, I begged the front desk clerk to call the police.

"Please, Miss. Can you call 911. I need help. My boyfriend kidnapped me and brought me here."

The clerk looked unfazed. "Ma'am, this goes on all the time. We are not allowed to call the police all the time for people. The police are tired of showing up here. Management said we can only call if we see something that warrants a call.":

"You don't understand. He is going to rape me and hold me here against my will. You have to call the police. Please!"

"Sorry, I can't," she said.

Just then, Vic walked back in and looked suspiciously at us. "What's going on here?"

I looked at the clerk with pleading eyes to do something. But she just pursed her lips and folded her arms.

"Xiyya! What is going on? Did you book the room? Come on, let's go!"

The clerk offered us a cheaper room. But Vic slammed the key down from the room we had earlier and told the clerk we wanted the same room — the more expensive room. He pulled on my jacket to bring me closer to him. Then he pulled my shirt and spun me around.

I let it all out. "Please!" I screamed. "He is going to hurt me. I have my little nephew in the car. Don't let him take me to a hotel room. I don't want to be here. I've been kidnapped."

The tears ran down my face as I begged for help. But the clerk just asked us to leave the lobby. I put the charger in my purse and saw the gun. It screamed freedom: freedom from abuse, freedom from my oppressor taking me where I didn't want to go, freedom from the life he had created for me which was no life at all.

I reached inside and pulled out the gun. Suddenly both clerks behind the desk screamed and one turned to run. I turned toward Vic but I could not see him. It was as if he had disappeared. I could not see him when the shot rang out.

Bang! went the shot. And thud — as Vic's body hit the ground.

Everyone started screaming, ducking, and crawling away. I reached for the phone on the counter and called my 18-year-old son.

"I shot Vic."

Chapter 9 – Prison Daze

"You need to spend time crawling alone through shadows to truly appreciate what it is to stand in the sun."

— *Shaun Hick*

* *

I later learned that I made several phone calls in that moment, calling person after person with the same news: I shot Vic. I still do not remember making any of those calls. I don't even know how I knew the phone numbers. But I had to have made the calls because my sisters and my son all came up to the hotel.

Just after the shot rang out and I lowered the gun, one of the clerks walked up to me. I remembered her from a previous day care my kids had gone to. She spoke quietly and gently.

"Xiyya, put the gun down."

I felt my hand lower and release the gun into my purse. The worker guided my nephew and I into a back room and had us sit down. But the reality of how my life had just changed was too much for me to keep still. I walked outside to get some air.

Shortly after, the police stormed the lobby with their guns drawn. I threw my hands in the air and dropped my purse. One officer cuffed me while the other grabbed my purse holding the weapon. They led me toward the squad car. I sat there is a daze. Thankfully, the police invited my son and sister over to talk to me. I was coming back to reality, but I was far from normal. As my sister and son bent over to talk to me through the window, the tears started to flow.

"What am I going to do?" I asked them again and again. "What am I going to do?"

When I first arrived in jail, I couldn't have been more terrified. I looked from the left to the right. I was in a cold, dark place both literally and figuratively. In jail, I felt that I was deaf and blind. My senses were dulled for the first weeks I was there. I wasn't sure if I was coming or going.

I was locked up for two years.

Chapter 10 – Court is in Session

"I managed to survive, when I could not run I did not stop walking, when I could not walk I did not stop crawling, and when I stopped crawling I searched for a spark to motivate myself to try again, to not give up for long!"

— *Shadi Kamal Kandil*

* *

..... I had to keep fighting. It was for the people and the places and the things I loved that I stayed alive. Nothing would ever be the same after I had been hurt so deeply, but to still have the courage to love—that was real bravery, the bravery people talked about in stories and tales."

— *Meara O'Hara, The Wanderess and her Suitcase*

* *

"It was cruel. Like opening a birdcage to let the bird fly out, whilst all the while it's tethered by the leg, and freedom is only an illusion."

— *Laini Taylor, Strange the Dreamer*

* *

Court was an absolute nightmare. My lawyer felt that I had an open and shut case of self-defense after years of abuse. But there was nothing open about my court proceedings. I had the judge from hell. She seemed predisposed to lock me away and throw away the key. My lawyer made motion after motion. She denied nearly everyone one. But my lawyer was tough. She was not afraid to go hard against the judge who made Judge Judy look like Mother Teresa.

Being in the courtroom was sheer torture, but the torture continued outside of the courtroom. A CPS case was opened immediately because my kids did not have parents. Their mother was in jail for who knew how long and their father/stepfather was dead.

The courts gave my 18-year-old custody of my other 5 kids. It seemed like a good idea at the time. The kids would all be able to stay together. But it got overwhelming for him in no time.

I could do nothing to help my son other than give him advice since I was rotting away in jail for two years fighting my case. My attorney was brilliant. She discovered that Vic had sent about fifteen pictures of me to an unknown person. My attorney said it looked like what someone would do when they wanted to put a hit out on someone.

It looked like we were getting a break in the case. I decided at that point that I was not going to let jail destroy me. Since I had to be there, I would make the most of the terrible situation. I started attending Bible classes. Then, it hit me that I could turn my pain into purpose. So, I held a domestic violence class. I met some good people and had a lot of ups and downs. I was able to talk to other women about what I went through and listen to their stories as well.

I got a notice from my attorney that CPS wanted me to sign my parental rights over. A lot of people didn't think I was ever coming home. They didn't believe that I could beat the charges. And after seeing how the judge had it out for me, who could blame them.

But I refused to sign over my parental rights. I continued to fight believing that one day I would get back home to my kids. With God on our side, we became a family again.

After sitting in jail for a year-and-a-half, I realized that I needed to deal with the trauma I had suffered. I signed up for different classes that would help me to learn how to identify the difference between healthy and unhealthy relationships and how to set boundaries that will help me become a better me.

The "no police call policy" that has been instituted at many hotels and motels has interrupted a lot of lives. People who could have been saved from abuse or worse were left to fate because the hotels were told by their management to do nothing. I wondered how my life would have been different if that clerk had agreed to pick up the phone and call 911. I asked both desk clerks — pleaded with them — for help. I even explained that I had been kidnapped by this man 4 to 5 times in the past. But they would not budge. Moments later, he was dead, and I was in custody.

I lost everything after my arrest. The abuse extended from me to my children and then to my family. Everyone suffered.

My attorney introduced evidence in the case that a lifetime no contact order was in place between us. Still, due to my personal failures and the failure of the many government systems, I sat in jail arrested and charged with his murder.

I was the suspect, true. But did anyone understand that I was also the victim?

I was charged with murder, but the state started getting nervous and worried that they couldn't make a murder one charge stick with so much evidence of domestic violence. They dropped the charge to manslaughter and aggravated battery a few days before the trial began. Still, I was facing decades in prison.

The trial lasted for three days. I was nervous with no idea what I would do if I was found guilty. There were days I thought suicide would be better than waiting. But my lawyer kept me encouraged. Her name was Katie Jackson, a sharp, Black woman who was not skilled in domestic violence cases, but a brilliant lawyer nonetheless. Despite her training and knowledge, she retained her street smarts and savvy about urban life.

We had a tough choice to make. Should I take the stand? It was a difficult call, but so many of the 50 witnesses on my witness list couldn't testify. Some of them didn't present well when my lawyer practiced with them in her office. My family would not do well as witnesses because of how they behaved in the courtroom. The bailiff had thrown so many of them out because they were praying or cheering.

My sister, Sharon, would come each day and pray in the courtroom. She would walk around putting blessed oil on the door handles and courtroom seats. My family gathered together in a prayer circle before court and after. For my part, I fasted and prayed.

There were days when I thought all hope was lost, especially as the state lined up witness after witness to make him look like an angel. I even thought about taking a plea that would have included a prison term. But Katie wasn't having any of that. She was confident in our defense and certain we would ultimately win, in spite of the constant barrage of obstacles the judge and defense team threw at us.

The judge was against me from the start. She denied a lot of my evidence and overruled my attorney's objections. But she let the state have free reign to submit as much evidence as they want. She sustained most of their objections.

For example, my attorney tried to explain that I needed to look presentable for court and told her how difficult it was to style black hair. She tried to explain that my hair needed a lot of work. There was no way to do it in jail to make it presentable for trial. She asked if we could have a stylist work on it in the back just before trial. But the judge said no.

In addition, many of my witnesses had been denied by the judge. But she couldn't deny me. We decided that I was my own best witness. Only I could testify about the horrors I had endured. But it was risky. My lawyer feared that if I choked, I would say something to make Vic sound sympathetic and paint myself as a cold-hearted killer.

But I did well. I showed all my scars, one-by-one, where he had hit me, kicked me, scratched me, and bit me. I pulled a fake tooth out of my mouth to show the jury where he had hit me so hard, he knocked it out.

His family also testified. But every time one of them would get on the stage, they had to admit that they did not recognize me. I looked so different in my suit. I looked like one of the lawyers. It wasn't until I testified that everyone knew who I was.

The trial lasted for three days. The jury deliberated for just 12 hours before returning their verdict. However, halfway through their deliberation, we were called back into the courtroom. One juror was having a major panic attack. She said she wanted to do what was right and find me guilty but there was too much pressure in the jury room. They were arguing and the lone juror just wanted out. She was released and the alternate juror was brought in to replace her. An hour later, they came in and rendered the verdict. My testimony plus the accounts of the hotel staff on the day I shot Vic were enough to win the day. I was found not guilty.

I was proud of Vic's family. They could have easily hated me for what I had done. But when I turned around at the end of the trial, I saw Vic's brother sitting next to my sister. He was gracious and said that his only wish was that Vic and I had stayed away from each other when he was alive.

I even had a chance to talk to his father. He sent me a copy of the obituary from the funeral and welcomed me to visit Vic's grave. It took herculean effort to find the gravesite. After checking records online, I finally found the spot.

At the gravesite, my children and I gathered around his tombstone. My children were surprisingly happy to see where he was laid to rest. My emotions were raw, but I felt no sadness. It was the period at the end of a long and sordid chapter of my life. We said our goodbyes and set off to put our lives back together.

Chapter 11 – Playing Games

"Don't play his game. Play yours."

— Rachel Caine, *Fall of Night*

* *

"The guarantee of safety in a battering relationship can never be based upon a promise from the perpetrator, no matter how heartfelt. Rather, it must be based upon the self-protective capability of the victim. Until the victim has developed a detailed and realistic contingency plan and has demonstrated her ability to carry it out, she remains in danger of repeated abuse."

— Judith Lewis Herman, *Trauma and Recovery: The Aftermath of Violence - From Domestic Abuse to Political Terror*

* *

I had to come to the realization that I was playing a dangerous game. It was a kind of emotional roulette. And any moment, the tables could have been turned and Vic could have been on the stand testifying about my murder while my body lay cold in the grave. As it was, I had lost everything.

When I was in jail, I was distraught. I didn't know if I was coming home or if I was going to spend 30 years of my life behind bars. I felt so much sadness, shame, and guilt. I was mad at myself. I was mad at Vic. I was mad at the world that I didn't love myself enough to run from a man like him. I wished I could turn back the hands of time and bring Vic back.

Then one night, he came to me in a dream. He said it was OK and that he forgave me. He told me to fight to get out of jail and go home to our kids. After that dream, I had no worries before the trial started. I believed I would be coming home. That is precisely what happened.

Once I was released, I couldn't wait to see my children and went to visit them as soon as I got out.

I slept in my truck the first night after being released from jail because I had nowhere to go. Even though I was free, it was like I was still in jail. I couldn't be with my children by court order until I had a job and a home. Thankfully, I was smart enough to save up money in jail. So, the next day. I rode around to find a place with the $2000 I had earned behind bars.

I found a great house that I thought would be perfect for my family. But the landlord told me that he had received about 70 phone calls about the house. I talked to him for a while, shared my story, and told him how desperately I needed the house if I was going to get my children back. That, and an extra month's rent as a deposit, helped me edge past the 70 others who wanted the house.

I had angels all around me helping me figuring out what my next steps were. Some I could not see — those Godsent invisible spirits who were there to help me. But others were angels in human form right here on earth. One was my therapist, Ms. Diedra who was very helpful when I got out. She furnished my whole house. She was a part of my life since I was pregnant with my eldest son, Robert, and continued to support me throughout my struggles.

Then my sister, Nicole, who owns a home health agency hired me. My kids were with me by the time I had a court date to get them back. Watching them running around the house being happy for the first time in a long time was a blessing to me. I remembered how the CPS workers tried to pressure me in jail to sign over my rights. I remembered how they tried to convince me that I would not win my court case. They kept telling me it was too expensive to keep the case open and I would save everyone a lot of money if I just gave up my rights. It was shameful behavior on their part.

While I am thankful that I was found not guilty and released from jail, my trip to hell was far from over. When I came home, it got real. I was diagnosed with PTSD. I was constantly sobbing. I started to have mild symptoms of paranoia and anxiety. I had to pile boxes and furniture against my back door to block it.

Sleep was the most difficult. I struggled to fall asleep and, when I did, I would awaken in terror. Silence was torture. Thankfully, my uncle lived with me. He was schizophrenic and made strange sounds all the time. But his disability turned out to be my blessing. They were like a lullaby to me. I slept peacefully if I could hear him making his noises.

He died a month before my son passed away. As I mourned his loss, I was also thankful that he was with me during those difficult early days after jail. He suffered greatly from his mental illness, but it served as a lifeline for me when I needed them most.

I went to the doctor for help. He put me on Zoloft to try to calm it down. But it didn't help. It took a year for my anxious mind to settle and let me return to normal.

My best advice to any woman who is in an abusive relationship is to run at the first sign. It won't get better. It won't change except to get even worse. Your love will not heal him. It will empower him to harm you more.

The first sign in my relationship was the day he spit on me. When he saw that I did not walk away after that, it made him bolder and made his abuse worsen over time.

The emotional mental abuse following the spitting. The way he talked to me grew more and more disrespectful. He would always throw in some good times in between the abuse to keep me coming back. The sex, the money, the vacations — they were all a tether to keep me back. Then, he started to hit.

As I look back, there were so many signs where I should have known we were in trouble. He even attacked me once at a funeral. A friend of mine had lost her child in a fire, and he went with me to the funeral. But he refused to come inside, choosing instead to wait outside. While I was sitting inside at the funeral, I heard shouting. It only took a minute before I realized it was his voice yelling for me to come outside so he could leave.

I know now that he was mentally ill though he was never diagnosed. Beyond that, he was immature. But he visited his own pain on me and on the children of the household until it broke us. One of my children paid the ultimate price.

My oldest son died just as I was beginning to write this book. He was shot and killed in a Waffle House. The cycle of violence and tragedy continued long after Vic was dead.

The big message from my life story is to love yourself. There can be no greater quest for any of us to embark on. When you have been the victim of domestic violence, you lose your sense of self, making it nearly impossible to love yourself properly.

Self-love is easy to talk about but hard to do especially when you don't see much about yourself that is loveable. Perhaps you have made a lot of mistakes over which you are ashamed. Maybe you have had someone in your life telling you that you are worthless. Or perhaps you have been beaten and battered so much that you think you aren't loveable.

The journey to healing is a path of accepting truths that you might struggle with at first. Acceptance is the key mantra here. Don't worry if you don't fully understand all of the things you need to accept. Just start slowly and know that, over time, things will become clearer and clearer.

Start by accepting (whether you believe it or not) that you do not deserve abuse. The person who hurts you is someone who doesn't love at all. They don't love themselves, so they can't love you. You don't deserve their abuse.

Next, accept that your abuser chose to hurt you. It is not your fault. You did nothing to cause it. He or she has toxic ways of processing life and took that all out on you.

Self-love that comes from a healthy place must start with practices of self-care. Taking care of you teaches you that you deserve care and respect. Follow these steps:

Listen to your heart.
Don't be afraid to spend a few moments in quiet and stillness to see what your heart is really saying.

Trust the fear of being alone.
It's OK to not be in a relationship until you are emotionally strong enough to do so. Being alone is not a tragedy. It is a triumph. It means that you love you and, once you are healed, you can offer yourself to someone else.

Silence all negative talk.
When you hear your brain saying something negative about yourself, counteract it with three positive things about yourself. Try repeating these mantras below. Don't worry if you don't believe them at first. You will as you continue to repeat them:

I am loving.

I am loveable.

I am beautiful.

I am powerful.

I deserve to be treated with respect.

I deserve compassion.

I am getting better every day.

Get busy
Rather than sit around worrying about being in a relationship, fill your life with your passions. Join a theater group. Get involved in church activities. Volunteer to coach a team. It doesn't matter what you do. Just do everything your heart and your interests lead you to.

Learn to trust your instincts
Your gut will tell you when people are no good for you. You must learn to trust that feeling. It is better to walk away from someone who is destructive than to learn it after years of relationship. Surround yourself with people who speak life to you rather than those who tear you down.

Chapter 12 – The Highest Price

"This is our purpose: to make as meaningful as possible this life that has been bestowed upon us . . . to live in such a way that we may be proud of ourselves, to act in such a way that some part of us lives on. This is our purpose: to make as meaningful as possible this life that has been bestowed upon us . . . to live in such a way that we may be proud of ourselves, to act in such a way that some part of us lives on."

— Oswald Spengler

* *

There are lots of ways in which you are paying a price when you allow yourself to be a victim of domestic violence.

- physical
- mental
- emotional
- spiritual

But one price of abuse seems too high to pay especially since you are not the one who has to pay it.

The biggest price of abuse is paid by your children. Their young minds are unable to process the heavy toll that abuse forces them to carry. And domestic violence brings with it generational curses. This is both a spiritual and a psychological truth. Children who live in homes where abuse is prevalent show a whole host of effects both in childhood and when they become adults.

My children have suffered mentally. Prior to the abuse, all of my children were attending magnet schools and were excelling academically. After the abuse, Vic's death, and my incarceration, my 9- and 13-year-old are attending a behavior management alternative school. My 10-year-old is attending a school inside of a mental hospital to deal with his emotional mental and behavior issues.

My godmother got custody of my children when I went to jail. The trauma turned them wild. My oldest sons, who were Vic's biological children, suffered the most. The eldest just started repeating, "I hate my Daddy. I hate my Daddy."

They are a little better now but are still having a lot of trouble. My youngest son gets suspended constantly because of behavior. Even though the schools were specially trained, they were not used to kids like mine.

We needed to make some changes. It started with a change of scenery when we moved from Indiana to Tennessee.

My family has suffered in every way possible: mentally, emotionally, socially, academically, and financially.

I never knew how real anxiety was until all of this happened. I am now a strong advocate for therapy for anyone who has come anywhere close to domestic violence. It harms everyone it touches. But it affects children most deeply because they are the least healthy.

I hope to change lives, save lives. But the lives who are most important are the lives of our children.

As we covered earlier, the biggest and most pronounced emotion kids feel is fear. That fear may show up as anger, a sense of terror, or a constant feeling of anxiety. That anxiety can surface at almost any time and without any provocation.

Kids who live with abuse live on guard and always feel that they are on the edge. That is because the eruptions that have happened in their home seem to come out of nowhere. They don't know or aren't present usually for all that leads up to a violent outburst. It can happen while they are playing, watching television, or even sleeping. To them, life feels wild and unpredictable and that makes children feel unsafe.

They don't allow themselves to wallow in happy thoughts and feelings because they have had their happiness interrupted by violence many times.

According to the United Way Children's Wellness Program, the reactions of kids can vary based on several factors. But the most prevalent factor is age. They say:

•   "Children in preschool. Young children who witness intimate partner violence may start doing things they used to do when they were younger, such as bed-wetting, thumb-sucking, increased crying, and whining. They may also develop difficulty falling or staying asleep; show signs of terror, such as stuttering or hiding; and show signs of severe separation anxiety.

•   School-aged children. Children in this age range may feel guilty about the abuse and blame themselves for it. Domestic violence and abuse hurts children's self-esteem. They may not participate in school activities or get good grades, have fewer friends than others, and get into trouble more often. They also may have a lot of headaches and stomachaches.

•   Teens. Teens who witness abuse may act out in negative ways, such as fighting with family members or skipping school. They may also engage in risky behaviors, such as having unprotected sex and using alcohol or drugs. They may have low self-esteem and have trouble making friends. They may start fights or bully others and are more likely to get in trouble with the law. This type of behavior is more common in teen boys who are abused in childhood than in teen girls. Girls are more likely than boys to be withdrawn and to experience depression."

When children are witnesses either through what they see and/or hear happening in the home, or because a parent is hospitalized or visually impacted in some way that children can see. For example, the child may be at school when the domestic violence occurred in the home. However, he or she may see black eyes, bruises, casts on arms, etc. Researchers have estimated that more than 3 million children in the United States witness some sort of incidents of domestic violence every year. In other countries, the numbers are believed to be even higher. But it is difficult to get accurate numbers in places like the Middle East where women's rights are nearly non-existent.

The long-term cognitive effect on children is well-documented. Many children display an inability to focus or concentrate. Their thinking feels muddled and clouded. Many children who are high performers in school show significant drops in their academic achievement.

Behavior is probably one of the first places where we witness changes that indicate a child is witnessing domestic violence. Children may become argumentative and be more prone to acts of physical aggression.

Emotionally, there are a whole host of behaviors that we see in children who witness violence in the home. These include anxiety, and depression. Children may regress to behaviors that comforted them earlier in life like thumb sucking or insisting on sleeping with a teddy bear or having the light on.

Externalized behaviors also seem to surface a lot when children have been exposed to this type of family violence. They may take on the role of the aggressor and start fighting, bullying others, lying to adults, or cheating in games or on tests. Or, they may take on the role of the victim with behaviors like fawning where they try to make everyone happy and do nothing to upset anyone. When asked what movie they want to see, for example, they are afraid to express an opinion and simply go along with the choices of others.

Children who witness violence struggle to socialize with their peers. We may see them having more conflicts at school or in the neighborhood with other children as well as with adults. Speaking of adults, defying authority is a common theme among children of domestic violence. They are less likely to work to resolve conflicts. They either shut down or go on the attack when a disagreement arises.

All of these behaviors are exacerbated by other demographic concerns. In other words, they tend to be more pronounced in homes that are dealing with other socioeconomic pressures like housing concerns, food shortages, and poverty.

Worst of all, because of sudden changes in the household, the children might miss many days of school or have to be moved to a different school because a parent is in jail or has been killed due to domestic violence. Child protective services often moves children far away from the neighborhood they know causing them to have to change schools as well.

In addition to separation from their parents, children have to deal with being "the new kid" in both a home and school setting.

Perhaps the most impacted are children who witness domestic violence but are then dragged into the violence. Many children are emotionally, sexually, and/or physically abused by the same person who victimized their abused paren. The child may feel it is his or her responsibility to jump into a physical altercation. As a result, they may be attacked by the aggressor or simply hurt in the fray.

Even infants are affected by domestic violence. According to the American Academy of Family Physicians:

> *The potential negative effects vary across the age span. In infants from homes with partner abuse, the child's needs for attachment may be disrupted.*

More than 50 percent of these infants cry excessively and have eating and sleeping problems. Infants are also at a significantly increased risk for physical injury.

The chart below shows how children might behave after witnessing domestic violence:

Age Span Differences - Potential Effects in Children Who Witness Violence*

AGE	POTENTIAL EFFECTS
Infants	Needs for attachment disrupted
	Poor sleeping habits
	Eating problems
	Higher risk of physical injury
Preschool children	Lack feelings of safety
	Separation/stranger anxiety
	Regressive behaviors
	Insomnia/parasomnias
School-aged children	Self-blame
	Somatic complaints
	Aggressive behaviors
	Regressive behaviors
Adolescents	School truancy
	Delinquency
	Substance abuse
	Early sexual activity

*—Effects categorized according to age. Information adapted from references.

Chapter 13 - Defining the Demon

To be clear, domestic violence is any experience of abuse that takes place in the home whether it is physical, psychological, or sexual abuse. Domestic violence occurs when one person attempts to use either of these three areas to assert control over the actions of another person.

Domestic violence ranks as a healthcare crisis in many countries including the United States. Awareness is increasing but not enough to stop abusers from abusing and women from accepting their roles as victims.

Most people know that domestic violence means hitting. But it includes so much more:

- Yelling
- Constant arguing
- Slapping
- Plucking
- Spitting
- Kicking
- Threatening suicide
- Threatening murder
- Intimidation
- Threats of violence
- Controlling

According to the Centers for Disease Control and Prevention, homes with violence between the adults result in a higher likelihood of child abuse. And as many as 80 percent of children who grow up around domestic violence report that they have witnessed it.

So, when you save yourself from domestic violence, you also save your children from it.

Here are the stats according to the CDC:

- On average, nearly 20 people per minute are physically abused by an intimate partner in the United States. During one year, this equates to more than 10 million women and men.
- 1 in 4 women and 1 in 9 men experience severe intimate partner physical violence, intimate partner contact, sexual violence, and/or intimate partner stalking with impacts such as injury, fearfulness, post-traumatic stress disorder, use of victim services, contraction of sexually transmitted diseases, etc.
- 1 in 3 women and 1 in 4 men have experienced some form of physical violence by an intimate partner. This includes a range of behaviors (e.g., slapping, shoving, pushing) and in some cases might not be considered "domestic violence." 1
- 1 in 7 women and 1 in 25 men have been injured by an intimate partner.
- 1 in 10 women have been raped by an intimate partner. Data is unavailable on male victims.
- 1 in 4 women and 1 in 7 men have been victims of severe physical violence (e.g., beating, burning, strangling) by an intimate partner in their lifetime.1
- 1 in 7 women and 1 in 18 men have been stalked by an intimate partner during their lifetime to the point in which they felt very fearful or believed that they or someone close to them would be harmed or killed.
- On a typical day, there are more than 20,000 phone calls placed to domestic violence hotlines nationwide.
- The presence of a gun in a domestic violence situation increases the risk of homicide by 500%.
- Intimate partner violence accounts for 15% of all violent crime.
- Women between the ages of 18-24 are most commonly abused by an intimate partner.

- 19% of domestic violence involves a weapon.
- Domestic victimization is correlated with a higher rate of depression and suicidal behavior.
- Only 34% of people who are injured by intimate partners receive medical care for their injuries.
- 1 in 5 women and 1 in 71 men in the United States has been raped in their lifetime.
- Almost half of female (46.7%) and male (44.9%) victims of rape in the United States were raped by an acquaintance. Of these, 45.4% of female rape victims and 29% of male rape victims were raped by an intimate partner.

ECONOMIC IMPACT

- Victims of intimate partner violence lose a total of 8.0 million days of paid work each year.
- The cost of intimate partner violence exceeds $8.3 billion per year.
- Between 21-60% of victims of intimate partner violence lose their jobs due to reasons stemming from the abuse.
- Between 2003 and 2008, 142 women were murdered in their workplace by their abuser, 78% of women killed in the workplace during this timeframe.
- Women abused by their intimate partners are more vulnerable to contracting HIV or other STI's due to forced intercourse or prolonged exposure to stress.
- Studies suggest that there is a relationship between intimate partner violence and depression and suicidal behavior.
- Physical, mental, and sexual and reproductive health effects have been linked with intimate partner violence including adolescent pregnancy, unintended pregnancy in general, miscarriage, stillbirth, intrauterine hemorrhage, nutritional deficiency, abdominal pain and other

gastrointestinal problems, neurological disorders, chronic pain, disability, anxiety and post-traumatic stress disorder (PTSD), as well as noncommunicable diseases such as hypertension, cancer and cardiovascular diseases. Victims of domestic violence are also at higher risk for developing addictions to alcohol, tobacco, or drugs.

This is the true verdict: domestic violence is real and real people are suffering from it every day.

Chapter 14 - Preventing Domestic Violence

Doctors, teachers, guidance counselors and other professionals can help to prevent domestic violence by being alert and aware of the signs, asking the right questions, and reporting their concerns to authorities.

But, in order for that to happen, schools and medical institutions need to educate their staff about the signs and what to look for. Though professionals have gotten better at noticing the primary victim (like the mother), they still struggle to acknowledge that children can be secondary victims of domestic violence.

Another concern in identifying domestic violence among professionals is understanding that it often does not take a physical form. Professionals who are looking for scars, broken limbs, and black eyes may miss the emotional abuse that often happens in families.

Children who, for example, witness constant arguments between their parents can have many of the same long-term effects of children who may witness striking.

A passion of mine is to help teens understand what healthy dating is long before they form lasting adult relationships. If we can teach girls (any boys) the essential lessons of loving themselves and demanding respect from their peers, we can help to avoid abuse early in life.

The American Academy of Family Physicians recommend the following questions on their website using an acronym called "FISTS":

Fighting: When was your last pushing-shoving fight?
How many fights have you been in during the past month?
The past year?

Injuries: Have you ever been injured in a fight?
Do you know anyone who has been injured or killed?

Sexual violence: What happens when you and your boyfriend
(or girlfriend) have an argument? Do you make up with sex?
Have you ever been forced to have sex against your will?

Threats: Have you ever been threatened with a knife? A gun?

Self-defense: How do you avoid getting in fights?
Do you carry a weapon for self-defense?

Helping Patients Plan for Safety
Do you feel safe going home? If not, where could you go?

Are you aware of your local resources?

Can you keep money, important papers, and telephone numbers in a
safe place?

Are there weapons in the home?

Can they be removed or placed in a safe, locked area?

Do you have a friend or family member with whom you can stay?

Chapter 15 – In Good Company

People stay in abusive relationships for all sorts of reasons:

- They have low self-worth
- Inability to support oneself alone.
- Fear of retribution
- Fear of being alone
- Need to save others
- Staying together for the children
- Shame of a breakup among friends and family

Domestic violence does not discriminate against age, gender, or ethnicity. It can even touch the rich and famous of the world. When celebrities are affected by domestic violence and are brave enough to share their stories, it benefits everyone by raising awareness and calling attention to an ongoing health crisis.

Several celebrities have come forward and confessed that they have been the victim of domestic violence. In so doing, they should know that it can happen to anyone. And they help give strength to fans who may be suffering.

Christina Aguilera

The pop star confessed that she experienced abuse at the hands of her father when she was a child. She told W Magazine:

> *"I felt caged by my childhood, and unsafe. Bad things happened in my home; there was violence."*

She acknowledged the impact domestic violence has on children and wished that her son would never experience it.

> *"I never wanted Max to be around arguing or unnecessary discomfort. I could be bitter about my childhood, but if anything, I'm thankful that I have that experience. I know my bigger purpose is to empower, to encourage other people to find their voice."*

She worked hard to overcome the trauma she experienced as a child. Among other things, she used yoga to aid in her healing:

> *"My whole life has been about 'fight or flight,' but yoga has helped me to appreciate the moment and be okay with the now."*

Aguilera is a strong advocate against domestic violence and has given money to charities that help victims.

Dwayne Haskins

Haskins is proof that domestic violence can also touch men. While women are the typical victims, men can also suffer from domestic violence. In fact, 25 percent of men report that they have suffered at the hands of their partners.

As a football player, namely a quarterback, for the Pittsburgh Steelers, it could not have been easy for Haskins to come forward. But he shared that his wife committed physical violence against him in a Las Vegas hotel. He alleges she punched him in the face and knocked out one of his teeth. Police arrived and took him to the hospital. His wife was arrested.

Halle Berry

Halle Berry is one of the most recognized women in entertainment. But she is also the child of a household where domestic violence was prevalent:

> *"For a good chunk of my childhood, my mother was a battered woman. Domestic violence can happen to anyone, including celebrities. It's not an issue of class or economics, it's whether you value yourself enough to expect better treatment."*

She states that her father battered her mother for all of Berry's childhood. And Berry was the one who suffered the emotional damage.

> *"I've struggled with self-worth problems. I never had to run to a shelter, but I have at times chosen the wrong partner, and I've run out the door if I suspected violence was possible."*

Berry continues to provide love and support to her mother who has escaped her abused:

> *"She's still struggling with why she put up with the abuse, and why she put her kids in that environment."*

Berry is a staunch supporter of the Jenesse Center, which provides shelter and support to victims and their children.

> *"I have an understanding, a knowing. I feel like I have something that I can impart to these women. It seems like I've overcome it, but I really haven't. In the quiet of my mind, I still struggle. So, while I'm*

helping these women, I'm helping myself through it, too."

Charlize Theron

She is a striking beauty and talented actress. She is also a survivor of domestic violence. Growing up in South Africa, she understands what it means to live in a place where women do not have equal rights.

Her father, who was an alcoholic, abused her mother. Theron's mother tried her best to protect her children from him. But one day, he came home drunk with a loaded pistol and began firing. Her mother was ready. She fired back and killed her abuser. Today, Theron serves as a United Nations "Messenger of Peace" in her quest to raise awareness and support victims.

Patrick Stewart

Stewart said his father was the victimizer in his life. All throughout childhood, his father filled the house with terror.

> *"As a child, I witnessed his repeated violence against my mother, and the terror and misery he caused was such that, if I felt I could have succeeded, I would have killed him."*

Stewart said that, when he was a child, domestic violence was not considered a crime. There was no one to turn to for help. Police would remark that his mother deserved the abuse she got because she "probably provoked" her husband. Steward was outraged by the comment even as a child.

> *"Nothing could be further from the truth. Violence is a choice a man makes, and he alone is responsible for it."*

Stuart raises money for "Refuge" — an organization that provides shelter and support for women and their children.

Rihanna

Few people missed the news that famous rapper, Chris Brown, battered his famous girlfriend, Rihanna. One might wonder how Brown thought that such an act against such a popular and beloved star would remain covered up.

Brown allegedly pushed Rihanna from a moving car after hitting her head against a window and punching her. Brown was arrested and charged with felony battery. He received just five years' probation and 180 days of community service. Rihanna laments that she, like many other women, took her abuser back. She had the restraining order removed that kept Brown away from her. The pair reconciled.

> *"I was that girl... That girl who felt that as much pain as this relationship is maybe I'm one of those people built to handle s*** like this. Maybe I'm the person who's almost the guardian angel to this person, to be there when they're not strong enough ... when they just need someone to encourage them in a positive way and say the right thing."*

She eventually removed herself from the relationship for good.

In honor of my mother, the following clippings of her murder and the subsequent investigation tell part of the sad story of her death and the impact of her loss on her family and the community.

THE INDIANAPOLIS STAR — WEDNESDAY, FEBRUARY 10, 1993

Body

★ Continued from Page 1

Nothing had turned up until Tuesday afternoon.

Andrew Charles, 28, and David Fitzpatrick, 21, were scavenging along the river and found a woman's body in a sandy area where the river had receded. The two men alerted nearby construction workers, who called police.

The body was found about 50 yards west of the river, south of I-465.

The body has yet to be identified by the Marion County coroner's office, officials stressed. Jackson's dental records probably will be used today in an attempt to identify the body.

Jackson's 12 children have been waiting for months to find out what happened to their moth-

er. In the past, they expressed ambivalence about believing Ditto's story.

On Tuesday, one of Jackson's daughters, Montique Anderson, said she would wait until she knows whether it's her mother before saying anything about the possible development in the case.

Indianapolis Police Detective Steven R. Guther said he has talked several times with Ditto, as recently as last week.

"He [Ditto] sounded remorseful" and was worried while waiting for Jackson's body to be found, Guther said.

Ditto had been released from jail uncharged on Dec. 3 because police could not find the victim's body. He had been arrested on a preliminary charge of murder.

"Without the body it would have been an extraordinarily difficult case to prove through circumstantial evidence," Marion County Prosecutor Jeffrey Modisett said Tuesday. "We began an investigation to get that necessary circum-

Police investigators remove a body, believed to be that of Rosa Pearl Jackson, along White River near I-465 on the Southwestside.

stantial evidence, and the case had been referred to the grand jury."

If the body is identified as Jack-

son, the case will be much easier to prove and charges will be filed immediately against Ditto, Modisett said.

SATURDAY, DECEMBER 5, 1992

POLICE BEAT

Ex-boyfriend confesses to pre-Thanksgiving killing

According to police reports, 51-year-old Robert Allen Ditto, has surrendered and confessed to killing his former girlfriend, 42-year-old Rosa Pearl Jackson.

Ditto, who resides in the 3200 block of East 39th Street told police he became upset while he and Jackson walked along the edge of the river, choked her and left her in the river. Police reports indicate Ditto became angry when Jackson informed him she had no plans on resuming their relationship, which family members said ended nearly five months ago. So far searches have not found the body of Jackson, and police report until the body is found, charges most likely will not be filed.

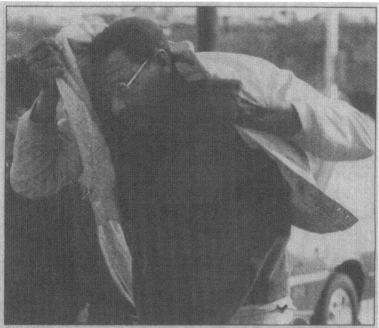

Mike Fander/The Indianapolis News

Robert Ditto tries to evade reporters and photographers after he was released from the Marion County Jail Thursday.

Mystery murder suspect freed

Police fail in river search to find reported drowning victim

By JEFF ZOGG
The Indianapolis News

Robert Ditto is a free man today because police can't find the body of the woman he confessed to drowning in the White River the day before Thanksgiving.

But his case will be referred to a Marion County grand jury and police may be keeping him under surveillance.

"We don't report everything we may be doing to keep an eye on him," said Marion County Prosecutor Jeffrey Modisett.

Ditto, 51, of the 3200 block of East 39th Street, turned himself in to police Nov. 28 saying he had gotten into an argument with his ex-girlfriend, began choking her, fell into the White River near Oliver Avenue with her and presumed she drowned.

Ditto was held until about 4 p.m. Thursday on a charge of murdering Rosa Pearl Jackson, 42, of the 2300 block of North Capitol Avenue.

Thursday, he rushed passed news photographers who waited outside the City-County Building for his release.

Members of Jackson's family, who hold out a hope that she is still alive somewhere, said they fear Ditto will harm them.

About 30 minutes after Ditto was released, a restraining order was filed ordering him to stay away from them.

"I don't know what to think. I believe they would have come up with a shoe, jacket or something," said Sharon Davis, 27, one of Jackson's daughters. "Right now we're hoping for a miracle."

Modisett explained Ditto could not be held without corroborating evidence for more than 72 hours.

"If the body shows up, we can file charges immediately," Modisett said.

He said a murder case could be tried without the victim's body, but the circumstantial evidence must be strong.

IPD homicide Detective Steve Guthier said Ditto's account has been mostly consistant with his investigation.

But investigators still need to examine Jackson's habits, plans, lifestyle, work attendence, customs, bank accounts and general habits before concluding she has disappeared.

"The longer we wait, the stronger the case gets," Modisett said.

Divers have combed the river, but found nothing near the site where Ditto said the drowning occurred.

Police have used helicopters to search for the body and an infrared camera that will detect heat generated from a decomposing body, said Capt. Chris Dahlke, commander of the Indianapolis Police Department's major case branch.

"It would be very helpful for anybody along the White River to keep their eyes open," Modisett said.

City man gets 8 years in ex-girlfriend's death

Superior Court Judge Webster L. Brewer sentenced Robert Ditto on Wednesday to the maximum eight-year prison term for involuntary manslaughter in the strangulation of his ex-girlfriend.

Ditto, 52, 3200 block of West 39th Street, was convicted Aug. 8 after a bench trial for murder stemming from the death of Rosa Pearl Jackson, 42, the day after last Thanksgiving. Brewer found Ditto guilty of the lesser offense of involuntary manslaughter.

Joyce Cothal, one of the victim's 12 children, told Brewer on Wednesday that Ditto "should get the maximum punishment for what he did to my family."

After Jackson disappeared last November, Ditto surrendered to police. He was in custody several days and then released because police could not find her body.

Ditto told investigators he and Jackson had been walking along White River. When Jackson said she wanted to end the relationship, he began to choke her and they fell into the river, Ditto said. He swam to shore, but she disappeared under the water.

Tuesday, December 1, 1994

Tim Halcomb/The Indianapolis News

Search for body

Indianapolis Police Department divers search for the body of Rosa Pearl Jackson along the west bank of White River near Oliver Avenue today. Jackson's ex-boyfriend, Robert Allo Ditto, 51, surrendered to police Saturday and admitted to choking Jackson and leaving her in the river. Moniquee Anderson, 25, reported her mother missing Friday morning.

Family friend David Lynch comforts Geraldine Davis, who learned Wednesday that the body of a woman found on the banks of White River was her mother, Rosa Pearl Jackson.

Body found along river identified as that of missing mother of 12

By SUSAN SCHRAMM
STAR STAFF WRITER

(article text illegible)

"We're only going af-
...st extreme cases here."

...the ordinance, police
...responsible for tracking
...nts or guardians.

A hearing on the ordinance is
set for 5 p.m. Feb. 17 before the
council's Public Safety and Criminal Justice Committee in Room
260 of the City-County Building.

Body found near river believed to be woman missing 2½ months

By SUSAN SCHRAMM
STAR STAFF WRITER

A body believed to be that of the missing Rosa
Pearl Jackson was found Tuesday on the bank of
White River, near where her alleged killer had told
police they would find her.

Although the identity of the body had not been
confirmed, police said clothing matched what Jackson, 42, was wearing when she disappeared the day
before Thanksgiving.

If an autopsy today confirms the body as Jackson,
officials said charges will be filed immediately against
Robert Ditto, 51, her ex-boyfriend.

Jackson left her Near-Northside home Nov. 25
with Ditto and was not seen again. Ditto surrendered
to police three days later, allegedly telling detectives
he had choked his former girlfriend and watched her
disappear in the river near Oliver Avenue.

Ditto was arrested and held in jail for several days
before authorities decided they lacked the evidence
— namely, Jackson's body — to charge him with
murder.

Police detectives, divers and boaters conducted
numerous searches in and around the river. The
state Department of Natural Resources has been
looking for her body in weekly patrols of the river.

74

Appendix 1 – Media Coverage

CRIME WATCH 8

Woman not guilty in shooting of boyfriend at motel; murder charge dismissed

by: Staff Reports. Posted: Aug 16, 2018 / 04:18 PM EST / Updated: Jul 17, 2019 / 03:17 PM EST

INDIANAPOLIS (WISH) — A 36-year-old Indianapolis woman had murder charges dismissed as a jury found her not guilty in a 2017 homicide at a motel.

Xiyya Jackson, 36, of Indianapolis was released from jail after being found not guilty of voluntary manslaughter and aggravated battery Wednesday in Marion Superior Court, Criminal Division 4. She had initially been charged with the murder of "Victor Landon" 32, in what police called domestic violence.

Indianapolis Metropolitan Police Department were called to a room at Budget 8 Inn, 6850 E. 21st St., near 21st Street and Shadeland Avenue, around 11:30 a.m. March 31, 2017. Jackson was accused of shooting her boyfriend in the head, police said, and a 3-year-old child was about a foot away during the shooting. The child was not injured.

According to court documents, Jackson and Landon had been together for about 10 years and Landon is the father of two of Jackson's six children. ... In 2017, Jackson told police that there had been domestic violence in the past with Landon and he also had kidnapped her before, according to the court documents. The two had been arguing prior to the shooting.

APRIL 1, 2017 BY NAPTOWN BUZZ

Murder Charge
Monday, April 3, 2017, 11:11 AM
Indianapolis Metropolitan Police Department (IMPD) Homicide Investigators have been informed that Victor Landon has died from injuries. Detectives will meet with the Marion County Prosecutor's Office to discuss and review new charges in this case.

Friday, March 31, 2017, 9:00 PM
Indianapolis Metropolitan Police Department homicide detectives investigate after a critically injured man is found shot inside a motel lobby.

Just before 11:30 a.m. on March 31, 2017, officers with the Indianapolis Metropolitan Police Department (IMPD) East District were sent to the 6800 block of East 21st Street to respond to a person shot. Officers quickly arrived and found lying on the motel lobby floor a 32-year-old man suffering from at least one gunshot wound. EMS personnel arrived and transported the victim to Sidney and Lois Eskenazi Hospital in critical condition. Due to the victim's injuries, currently believed to be life-threatening, the victim's name is not being released.

East District officers quickly apprehended a female later identified as 34-year-old Xiyya Jackson nearby the scene. Witnesses told officers that Xiyya Jackson was the shooter of the critically wounded man. The suspect was taken to IMPD Homicide Office to be questioned by homicide detectives. After being questioned by detectives they arrested the suspect on a preliminary criminal charge of attempted murder. Detectives also recovered from the suspect a handgun believed used by the suspect. The suspect was transported to the Arrestee Processing Center to be processed and booked on a criminal offense. In the coming days detectives plan to review their investigative findings with the Marion County Prosecutor's Office for a charging decision.

Detectives have not yet released the relationship between the suspect and victim, but they do not believe the shooting was random; nor have they indicated if this shooting is believed to be domestic related. Once additional details are known, or the victim's condition worsens this news release will be updated with new and relevant information.

SOURCE: Indianapolis Metropolitan Police Department

Appendix 2 - Resources For Battered Women & Book Sources

According to LMF Therapist, Blake Edwards, the best way to support a person who is being abused is to follow these simple tips:

- "Don't judge the person who is being abused.
- Avoid telling the victim that they need to leave. Instead, discuss a safety plan.
- Don't tell the victim that the abuser is a jerk. That could drive the victim away or make them feel like they have to defend their abuser.
- Become the victim's confidante. Listen to everything they tell you. If they go to the authorities about the abuse, you could be a good witness later by backing up their story.
- Assure the person that they can speak to you in confidence, and that you can help them through it.
- Teens experiencing domestic violence in a romantic relationship can text "loveis" to 22522 to get help via text from LoveIsRespect.org, a resource that empowers young people to prevent and end dating abuse.
- If you're experiencing abuse, consider telling your primary care doctor or a mental health professional who can help.
- If a child is witnessing domestic violence, know that this is a form of child abuse, and you must report it to the authorities.
- Suggest that the victim — and the perpetrator, if possible — seek mental health support."

National Resources for the Prevention of Domestic Violence
National Domestic Violence Hotline: 800-799-SAFE (7233)
National Resource Center on Domestic Violence: 800-537-2238
Family Violence Prevention Fund: www.fvpf.org

American Medical Association: www.ama-assn.org

American Academy of Pediatrics: www.aap.org

American Academy of Family Physicians: www.familydoctor.org

SOURCES

Brown, B., and Bzostek, S. (2003, August). Violence in the lives of children. Crosscurrents, 1. Bethesda, MD: Child Trends. Retrieved from http://www.childtrends.org/wp-content/uploads/2003/01

Carlson, B.E. (2000). Children exposed to intimate partner violence: Research findings and implications for intervention. Trauma, Violence, and Abuse, 1 (4), 321-342.

Edleson, J. (2011). Emerging responses to children exposed to domestic violence. Harrisburg, PA: VAWnet, a project of the National Resource Center on Domestic Violence/Pennsylvania Coalition Against Domestic Violence. Retrieved from http://www.vawnet.org/Assoc_Files_VAWnet/AR_ChildrensEx posure.pdf.

Hughes, H. M., Graham-Bermann, S. A., and Gruber, G. (2001). Resilience in children exposed to domestic violence. In S. A. Graham-Bermann (Ed.). Domestic violence in the lives of children (pp. 67-90). Washington, DC: American Psychological Association.

Kilpatrick, K.L., Litt, M., and Williams, L.M. (1997). Post-traumatic stress disorder in child witness to domestic violence. American Journal of Orthopsychiatry, 67 (4), 639-644.

Siegel, D., and Hartzell, M. (2004). Parenting from the inside out: How a deeper self-understanding can help you raise children who thrive. New York, NY: Tarcher.

Kantor, J. (2016). Seeing abuse, and a pattern too familiar: Janay Palmer, Ray Rice's wife, implied the assault was taken out of context. New York Times. Retrieved from: http://www.nytimes.com/2014/09/10/us/seeing-abuse-and-a-pattern-too-familiar.html?_r=0

Cravens, J. D., Whiting, J. B., & Aamar, R. (2015). Why I stayed/left: An analysis of voices of intimate partner violence on social media. Contemporary Family Therapy. DOI 10.1007/s10591-015-9360-8.

Whiting, J. B., Oka, M. & Fife, S. T. (2012). Appraisal distortions and intimate partner violence: Gender, power, and interaction. Journal of Marital and Family Therapy. doi: 10.1111/j.1752-0606.2011.00285.x

Barnett, O. W., Miller-Perrin, C. L., & Perrin, R. D. (2011). Family violence across the lifespan: an introduction (3rd ed.). Thousand Oaks, CA: Sage.

Johnson, M. (2008). A typology of domestic violence: Intimate terrorism, violent resistance, and situational couple violence. Boston: Northeastern University Press.

Merchant, L. V., & Whiting, J. B. (in submission) Factors in couples' desistance from domestic violence.

Brown, B., and Bzostek, S. (2003, August). Violence in the lives of children. Crosscurrents, 1. Bethesda, MD: Child Trends. Retrieved from http://www.childtrends.org/wp-content/uploads/2003/01/2003

Carlson, B.E. (2000). Children exposed to intimate partner violence: Research findings and implications for intervention. Trauma, Violence, and Abuse, 1 (4), 321-342.

Edleson, J. (2011). Emerging responses to children exposed to domestic violence. Harrisburg, PA: VAWnet, a project of the National Resource Center on Domestic Violence/Pennsylvania Coalition Against Domestic Violence. http://www.vawnet.org/Assoc_Files_VAWnet/AR_ChildrensExposure.pdf.

Hughes, H. M., Graham-Bermann, S. A., and Gruber, G. (2001). Resilience in children exposed to domestic violence. In S. A. Graham-Bermann (Ed.). Domestic violence in the lives of children (pp. 67-90). Washington, DC: American Psychological Association.

Kilpatrick, K.L., Litt, M., and Williams, L.M. (1997). Post-traumatic stress disorder in child witness to domestic violence. American Journal of Orthopsychiatry, 67 (4), 639-644.

Siegel, D., and Hartzell, M. (2004). Parenting from the inside out: How a deeper self-understanding can help you raise children who thrive. New York, NY: Tarcher.

https://www.aafp.org/afp/2002/1201/p2052.html#afp20021201p2052-b3

MELISSA M. STILES, M.D., University of Wisconsin-Madison Medical School, Madison, Wisconsin

Am Fam Physician. 2002 Dec 1;66(11):2052-2067

As we work to break the cycle of misfortune and generational curses, I want to memorialize those in my family who have died tragically.

My mother, Rosa, died in 1992. Her body was found in 1993 in the White River where it had been thrown. She had been murdered by her ex-boyfriend.

My sister, Montquee, died in February 2001 in an apartment fire. She was asleep when the fire broke out. She was known to cook Sunday dinner to feed anyone who stopped by wanting to eat. Sadly, she fell asleep with her dinner cooking, igniting the fire.

My sister, Vickie, was stabbed in August 2018 over 50 times the day after I was released from jail.

My nephew, London, was murdered when he was shot on October 28, 2018 at a Halloween party.

My sister, Jannie — nicknamed Grandma — died of an overdose on February 24, 2019.

My uncle, Daryl, died of an overdose. I found him dead on my kitchen floor on February 10, 2021.

My son, Robert — nicknamed Lil' Boo — was shot and killed at a Waffle House on March 25, 2021.

Help others find this book by leaving a review on the site where you bought it. Thank you!

Made in the USA
Middletown, DE
28 June 2022